Discover the full pot
Ripple & XR

Advantages - Vision - Investing - Community

Arndt Podzus

ISBN 978-3-9821446-2-7 (EBook)
ISBN 978-3-9821446-3-4 (Paperback)

First edition 2019

to my kids, for giving me purpose

to you, for giving it a chance

Disclaimer

All contents of this publication are for information and entertainment purposes only and do not constitute investment advice or an invitation to buy or sell the crypto-currencies and digital assets mentioned. It is exclusively a matter of subjective and non-binding statements on market conditions and individual investment instruments. Transactions with crypto-currencies and other digital assets involve risks that can lead to a total loss of the invested capital and beyond. Before you make an investment decision, you should obtain detailed advice on the risks of loss at a suitable point in time. Despite intensive research, errors may be contained. The author excludes liability claims of any kind.

All brand names and trademarks mentioned and, if applicable, those protected by third parties are subject without restriction to the provisions of the applicable trademark law and the rights of the respective registered owners.

This publication contains links to external websites of third parties, over whose contents the author has no influence. Therefore, the author cannot assume any liability for these external contents. The respective provider or operator of the sites is always responsible for the contents of the linked sites. The linked pages were checked for possible legal violations at the time of linking. Illegal contents were not recognizable at the time of linking.

However, a permanent control of the contents of the linked pages is not reasonable without concrete evidence of a violation of the law. Upon becoming aware of any infringements, the author will remove such links from the publication.

Content

Introduction

This book is written for all those, who out of interest in investing in cryptocurrencies or out of fascination with the possibilities of blockchain technology, would like to find out about another exciting alternative to Bitcoin and Ethereum. You do not need any detailed technical knowledge. For the purchase and secure storage of cryptocurrencies you should know how to use a computer and know the related terminology.

This book is aimed at technically experienced non-professionals who, out of interest in cryptocurrencies or out of fascination with the possibilities of blockchain technology, would like to find out about other exciting alternatives besides Bitcoin and Ethereum.

After reading this book, you will understand why the establishment of a new global financial infrastructure by *Ripple* is only the first step of a mission on which they are already further than many people think. The real vision, however, is the realization of the Internet of Value, where any value can be sent around the world as quickly and cheaply as information can be sent today.

You will recognize the importance and potential of the crypto currency *XRP* for the realization of this vision and also that *XRP* will benefit in the long run from every existing (e.g. also Bitcoin) and every new digital currency (e.g. issued by states or even Facebook Libra) rather than competing.

You will also learn how and where you can buy *XRP* easily and directly against EURO, US Dollar or many other FIAT currencies and what you have to consider.

Finally, I will introduce you to other companies and services that are already working on the vision of the *Internet of Value* and you will meet important people in the *XRP community* who are an ideal starting point to delve further into the subject.

But before I start, I would like to explain the important difference between *Ripple* and *XRP*, briefly introduce the

Blockchain technology and show you reasons why cryptocurrencies are becoming more and more attractive.

What is the difference between Ripple and XRP?

Although both are often still used synonymously, this is not correct. *Ripple* is a Fintech company with headquarters in California[1] and *XRP* is a crypto currency and a digital asset and a so-called utility token that resides on a **public ledger**[2], the **XRP Ledger**[3]. The XRP Ledger is based on open source technology. This means that anyone can view it, use it or suggest changes.[4] It's not owned by *Ripple*.

There are now various developers who create software based on the XRP Ledger. I will introduce some of them later.

The reason for the frequent synonymous use of *Ripple* and *XRP*, lies in the history of the development of the XRP-Ledger,

---

1   https://www.ripple.com/company/
2   Public ledger means that all transactions and accounts are publicly accessible pseudonymously
3   David Schwartz, CTO at Ripple, March 2018
    https://www.quora.com/What-is-the-difference-between-XRP-XRP-Ledger-and-Ripple
4   https://github.com/ripple/rippled

the originally involved developers, who worked for Ripple and the fact that Ripple was the only company, which advanced the development of the XRP-Ledger for a long time. I will not go into further details in this introduction. I will also refrain from technical details, e.g. what the difference is between **Blockchain** and **Distributed Ledger Technology (DLT)** or between a cryptocurrency, a digital asset and a utility token. You do not need to know these technical or definitional details to understand or invest in the potential of the technology and use cases. The terms are often used synonymously.

Blockchain and cryptocurrencies

There is hardly a company that has not experimented with blockchain technology or even already realized applications. It is used in the following areas, for example:

- For supply chains (supply chain management),
- in logistics processes,
- in the areas of accounting, finance and controlling,
- in production processes,
- and so on...

to name just a few.[5] When it comes to the use of a cryptocurrency, the media usually only talk about **Bitcoin** or sometimes **Ethereum**. Bitcoin appears more often in the news when it comes to the seizure of the same in connection with illegal activities in the so-called **Darknet**.[6]

Recently, one also hears more often about digital currencies, such as Facebook Libra or digital currencies planned by states.[7] The big difference here is that they are not decentralized, but centrally controlled and therefore have a so-called counterparty risk, which can lead to the same confidence problem in international trade as with today's fiat currencies. FIAT currencies are money that is issued by a country's central bank and traded as a legal, officially recognized medium of exchange.[8]

---

5   Blockchain in Germany - use, potentials, challenges, study report 2019, https://www.bitkom.org/sites/default/files/2019-06/190613_bitkom_studie_blockchain_2019_0.pdf)
6   The Darknet is a largely anonymous and isolated area of the Internet, which can only be accessed via a specific access.
7   https://boerse.ard.de/anlageformen/kryptowaehrungen/kommt-der-digitale-EURO-fuer-alle100.html, retrieved: 10.12.2019
8   https://coinvestoren.com/fiat-waehrungen, retrieved: 12.12.2019

It may surprise some people that there are already 4,890 crypto currencies.[9] Not all of them have any real benefit and some of them only exist to take money out of the pockets of inexperienced investors. A good approach to evaluating individual crypto currencies is to look at the answers to the questions:

Does this solve a concrete problem better than before?
How big is the problem?

If it is just the next cryptocurrency that claims to be the next world currency, it can be safely ignored.

A problem that the Fintech company *Ripple*, for example, wants to solve with the crypto currency and the digital asset *XRP* is about 5.7 trillion dollars - per day - and the future development potential is only limited by one's own imagination. The next chapters will tell you what this problem is and what this has to do with imagination.

---

9   https://coinmarketcap.com/, Stand: Dezember 2019

Why are cryptocurrencies becoming more and more attractive?

Slow and expensive international transactions

There are several reasons why cryptocurrencies such as Bitcoin were created. On the one hand, this was due to the increasing maturity of the Internet. In a globalized world, which was brought ever closer together by the Internet, it also makes sense to have a common global currency, because existing possibilities for international transactions were expensive and slow and are still common today.

The 2008 financial crisis

The second reason was probably the 2008 financial crisis, which mercilessly exposed the weaknesses of our global financial system and showed how individual actors in that system can cause huge global damage through greed. The first highlight of the financial crisis was the collapse of the investment bank *Lehman Brothers* on September 15, 2008.[10]

---

10   https://www.zeit.de/zeit-magazin/2018/37/finanzkrise-2008-lehman-brothers-investmentbank-pleite-auswirkungen, retrieved: 10.12.2019

Without now going into all the details of the financial crisis or giving a detailed account of the economic context, one can see an origin in too much cheap money in the markets, i.e. too much money that central banks had printed to boost domestic consumption. This kept interest rates low, which led many people in the U.S. to borrow on consumer goods, especially real estate, that they could not actually afford. Many bankers knew this. Nevertheless, these bad real estate loans were tied up in alleged **Triple A**[11] packages and sold to other financial institutions worldwide via funds. When interest rates rose slightly and property prices fell at the same time, many of these loans burst and billions had to be written off worldwide. This ultimately led to the bankruptcy of *Lehman Brothers* and threatened to drag other financial institutions worldwide into the abyss. Only with the help of government rescue packages could many banks, which were described as "systemically relevant", be saved. The world slid into recession, the banks became more cautious and no longer trusted each other. As a result, they granted less credit and private consumption

---

11   high credit rating, high security for capital repayment, very low risk for investors

13

declined accordingly.

Creditor participation (*bail-in*)

In order to compensate for this, interest rates were lowered more and more. Greece, already heavily indebted, was threatened with bankruptcy and could only be saved from this by the EU. The next highlight was the bail-in of investors in the Cyprus crisis in March 2013. Without this, the EU states would not have been able to prevent the collapse of the Cypriot banking system and the threat of state bankruptcy. Without law and without their consent, investors were involved in the restructuring of the banks by cutting their claims by up to 50 percent. To put it in clear terms: anyone who had more than 100,000 EUROs in their bank account was partially deprived of it.[12]

This is exactly what can happen in the entire EU since 2016. In the meantime, probably every European and U.S. bank has anchored this creditor participation in its general terms and

---

12   https://www.spiegel.de/wirtschaft/soziales/zypern-krise-wie-sich-das-land-
     seinen-banken-ausgeliefert-hat-a-889845.html, retrieved: 10.12.2019

conditions.[13] So if you have more than e.g. 100,000 EUROs in an account, I would think twice about it. Since the new trend is also negative interest rates (defacto money devaluation), it is becoming increasingly unattractive to hoard money in an account.

Meanwhile we are trapped in a vicious circle. Because it costs almost nothing to borrow money, but at the same time there is little, no or even negative interest on deposits, capital is fleeing into supposedly attractive forms of investment, such as real estate and stocks, which has led to an explosion in real estate and stock prices. Since any significant interest rate hike by central banks in the foreseeable future would probably lead to a collapse of the financial system, more and more cheap money continues to be printed, which will not increase confidence in the financial markets in the long run.

This lack of trust in the financial markets, participating banks, the fear of a bail-in, horrendous real estate prices and the

---

13   Example bail-in at Deutsche Bank, https://www.deutsche-bank.de/content/dam/
      deutschebank/de/shared/pdf/ser-bankenabwicklung-und-
      glaeubigerbeteiligung.pdf, retrieved: 10.12.2019

search for alternative attractive forms of investment have significantly increased the attractiveness of alternative forms of investment, such as cryptocurrencies, in recent years. However, many people also hoard their cash at home, especially among the older generation.

Cryptocurrencies such as *Bitcoin* or *XRP* are based on a decentralized system (peer-to-peer transactions). There is no central instance and no central server over which the transactions run (i.e. no counterparty risk). All transactions are final, cryptographically encrypted, cannot be manipulated afterwards and are transparent to everyone. However, it is not possible to see which person made a transaction, but only which addresses (accounts) were involved. It is therefore pseudonymous, but not anonymous.

Chapter 1: Why XRP and Bitcoin do not compete?

As already mentioned in the introduction, I currently see the greatest future potential of all cryptocurrencies known to me in *XRP*. I will now go into the reasons in detail. However, one must keep in mind that Bitcoin and *XRP* have completely different original use cases. While Bitcoin positions itself as a global currency and store of value, *XRP* positions itself as a complement to the existing financial system. It is intended to be used as a bridge currency, which enables the effective and efficient exchange between different currencies, cryptocurrencies and other values in real time. I will discuss this in detail below.

In order to show transparently why I think *XRP* has great potential, especially from an investor's perspective, I analyze and evaluate *Bitcoin* and *XRP* according to the following criteria:

- Market positioning & potential
- Performance
- Legal framework
- Team, consultants, partnerships
- Community & Marketing

Market positioning and potential of Bitcoin vs. XRP

Bitcoin (BTC or sometimes abbreviated as XBT) was positioned by its supporters from the beginning as an alternative payment system and store of value without a superior instance. In other words, as its own central bank, so to speak. Unlike existing central banks, it is not centrally controlled and cannot be politically influenced. Whether it fulfills all the functions of money is controversial, especially in the banking environment. The theoretical market potential is the processing of all global payments via Bitcoin and the value retention function.

Since the XRP Ledger (like Bitcoin) is open source, the market potential results from the combined market potential of the companies using the protocol and *XRP*. *XRP* is a cryptographically secured digital asset located in the *XRP Ledger* (**XRPL**).[14] The *XRP Ledger* is a distributed system for the efficient real-time transactions of any value. It has a fully integrated currency exchange. What this means in detail, I will explain in a moment. Currently, the main user of the *XRP Ledger* is still the company *Ripple*.

The name *XRP* is no coincidence. Currency codes are formed according to certain standards. Usually three letters, by adding a single character to the two-digit country code of the issuing country. Since the United States country code is "US", US dollars have the currency code "USD". The EU has the country code "EU", so the currency code for EURO is "EUR". Of course *XRP* is not issued by any country. For assets that are not issued by a country, the first letter must be X. For example, the chemical symbol for gold is "Au", so the currency code for gold is XAU. The "RP" comes from the name "Ripples", as the *XRP* were called in the early days. Some also call the *XRP*

---

14   https://xrpcommunity.blog/ripple-xrp-101/, retrieved: 08.12.2019

today **"ZERPS"**.[15]

Ripple positions *XRP* as a processing instrument for international payments, in line with its **RippleNet** payment platform. *Ripple* describes RippleNet as "a global network of banks and payment service providers using Ripple's distributed financial technology that enables real-time messaging, clearing and settlement of financial transactions".[16] *RippleNet* is based on an early version of the **Interledger Protocol (ILP)**[17] - an open, neutral protocol that enables cooperation between different ledgers and payment networks[18] *XRP* can be used as a settlement asset within RippleNet, but does not have to be. In theory, it can be any other currency, such as US dollars or even *Bitcoin*. But *XRP* offers a few advantages, which I will discuss below. *RippleNet* cannot exist without *Ripple* the company's software. The *XRP Ledger* and native *XRP* asset are independent of *Ripple* and *RippleNet* and would continue to exist with or without *Ripple* and *RippleNet*.

---

15   David Schwartz, Ripple, https://qr.ae/TZw3Rf, retrieved: 08.12.2019
16   https://ripple.com/files/ripplenet_brochure.pdf, retrieved: 08.12.2019
17   Ripple played a key and leading role in the development of the ILP, https://interledger.org/
18   https://ripple.com/files/xcurrent_brochure.pdf, retrieved: 08.12.2019

In summary, *XRP* is something quite different from Bitcoin. Realistically, Bitcoin's potential lies primarily in the store of value function. It is not suitable as a daily means of payment, as I will explain below. The *XRP Ledger*, on the other hand, is a **backend infrastructure** and is not actually designed as a product for the consumer (although it would be theoretically and practically possible). The *XRP Ledger* is a distributed real-time payment protocol for anything of value. It is a shared public database with an integrated distributed currency exchange, and is the world's first universal translator for money and other assets. The *XRP Ledger* is currency independent. The algorithm always finds the best way to transfer a value.[19] He can convert EUROs to US Dollars or bonus miles to Bitcoin. *XRP* can act as a bridge currency, as it is the fastest and cheapest way to make the transaction. For example, if you want to send USD to Mexico, it is first automatically converted to *XRP* and then automatically converted to Mexican Pesos at the destination. The whole thing happens within four seconds and

---

19   Tiffany Hayden, https://medium.com/@haydentiff/what-is-ripple-
      efc179bc02ae

costs fractions of a cent. External currencies are the focus of the protocol - not *XRP*. Since *RippleNet* is primarily a payment network, *XRP* is used for optimal liquidity management.[20] *Ripple* itself calls this **On Demand Liquidity (ODL)**.[21]

Ripple has already convinced over **300 companies** to use *RippleNet*.[22] These include well-known companies such as **American Express, Santander** and **Moneygram**. Moneygram, for example, already uses the On Demand Liquidity with *XRP*. The software is built in a way that a changeover to ODL is very easy possible.

This shows the basic market potential, at least for the first applications of *Ripple*. You currently have two specific markets in mind:

1. Nostro accounts

---

20   Tiffany Hayden, https://medium.com/@haydentiff/what-is-ripple-efc179bc02ae

21   https://ripple.com/wp-content/uploads/2019/09/RippleNet-On-Demand-Liquidity.pdf, retrieved: 14.12.2019

22   https://www.ripple.com/customers, retrieved: 05.12.2019

In total, more than 27 trillion dollars are stuck in so-called nostro accounts. Nostro accounts are held by banks for their current payments among themselves. They must be kept in all possible currencies and tie up capital in banks worldwide. Tied up capital accounts for more than 80% of payment costs. Ripple's goal is to free up this capital by requiring banks to maintain only one *XRP* account instead of many different nostro accounts, which would provide liquidity for all international transactions. At the same time, banks or other internationally operating companies avoid using the more expensive and slower **SWIFT system** or **SWIFT gpi**[23]. In 2018, the volume of money transferred amounted to around USD 300 billion per day[24], with an average of 31 million messages (transactions) per day[25]. One can therefore also say that Ripple wants to complement the SWIFT system, if not even replace it, as **Brad Garlinghouse**, the CEO of *Ripple*, has

---

23 SWIFT manages transactions between some 11,000 banks, brokerage houses, stock exchanges and other financial institutions in about 200 countries[2] via SWIFT messages

24 Swift GPI payments: over 3,500 banks with more than $40 trillion transactions in 2018, it-finanzmagazin.de, retrieved: 10.12.2019

25 https://www.pymnts.com/news/b2b-payments/2019/financial-messaging-cross-border-transactions/, retrieved: 05.12.2019

also confirmed.[26]

To understand it, it is important to note that SWIFT is primarily a messaging system, which means that when a transaction is made, only a message is sent to the recipient with the information about the transaction. The actual clearing and settlement, i.e. the balancing of accounts, usually takes place afterwards for international payments. The SWIFT system cannot provide 365/24/7 real-time liquidity in the way that *Ripple* can do with *XRP*.

2. Global Settlement

The second focus is on the global currency market. The foreign exchange market is the largest financial market in the world, with a global daily turnover of approximately $6.6 trillion in 2019.[27]

---

26 https://www.bloomberg.com/news/articles/2018-11-13/ripple-is-destined-to-overtake-swift-banking-network-ceo-says, retrieved: 05.12.2019

27 Bank for International Settlements: Turnover of OTC foreign exchange instruments, by currency, development of average turnover per trading day on the global foreign exchange market from 1989 to 2019 (in billion US dollars),

The market potential is also reflected in Ripple's vision of establishing the **"Internet of Value"**, in which values are moved around the world like information is already today.[28]

Unlike Bitcoin, which actively opposes the banks and regulators, Ripple proactively works with regulators worldwide. The latter should be much more promising. It is probably easier to improve the financial system from within than to oppose it completely. How likely is it that Bitcoin will succeed in replacing the current financial system without a central authority, without active stakeholder management and without targeted marketing from a decentralized position?

But there are other arguments in favor of XRP, which I will now discuss in the analysis of performance.

---

retrieved: 05.12.2019
28 https://www.ripple.com/company, retrieved: 05.12.2019

What are the important differentiators between XRP and Bitcoin?

Without going into somewhat emotional discussions about "better" or "more decentralized" technology, I will focus on the following measurable facts.

- Transaction speed
- Transaction fees
- Scalability
- Power consumption / CO_2 emissions

Transaction speed

Payments that move through the *XRP Ledger* take about four seconds.[29] With Bitcoin, the confirmation time of a transaction depends on the fees you are willing to pay for the transaction and the current network load. It is usually at least ten minutes, but can also be several hours. At the time of the last hypes in December 2017 the confirmation time for a transaction was sometimes 1-2 days.[30] For example, if Bitcoin is used in daily shopping for a coffee-to-go, the seller has to wait quite a long

---

29   https://ripple.com/xrp/, retrieved: 05.12.2019
30   https://coinsutra.com/bitcoin-transfer-time/, retrieved: 05.12.2019

time before he knows that he has received the money.

Transaction fees

With XRP, transaction fees can be a minimum of 0.00001 XRP[31] (10 drops[32]) and most people pay around 0.000015 XRP, which is negligible at a current price of 0.19 EUR per XRP. The fee is intended exclusively as a spam defence.[33] When a transaction is performed in the *XRP Ledger*, the transaction fee is destroyed. The number of *XRP* is therefore slightly deflationary.

With Bitcoin, transaction fees are variable and depend on the load on the network and the time you are willing to wait. You can view the currently recommended transaction fees[34] online.[35] At present they are at 0.00062 BTC (62 Satoshis[36]) per

---

31 https://xrpl.org/transaction-cost.html#current-transaction-cost, retrieved: 05.12.2019
32 Ein Drop ist die kleinste Einheit eines XRP (0,000001 XRP) und entspricht Einmillionstel XRP (1/1.000.000)
33 David Schwartz, Ripple, https://twitter.com/JoelKatz/status/949886637198082049, retrieved: 05.12.2019
34 https://btc.com/stats/unconfirmed-tx, retrieved: 05.12.2019
35 https://btc.com/stats/unconfirmed-tx, retrieved: 05.12.2019
36 Ein Satoshi ist die kleinste Einheit eines BTC (0,00000001 Bitcoin) und entspricht Einhundertmillionstel (1/100.000.000) eines Bitcoin.

transaction, which corresponds to approximately EUR 4.10 or USD 4.54. In December 2017, Bitcoin transaction fees reached 40 to 50 US dollars, so that transactions with low fees such as 1 to 10 US dollars had no chance of going through.[37] The level of the transaction fee makes Bitcoin unattractive for micropayments.

Additional transaction fees are charged by crypto exchange providers and other service companies as part of their business model. These vary widely, so it makes sense to check them out before taking up an offer.

Scalability

All *XRPs* already exist, so that unlike *Bitcoin*, there is no longer any effort for the computationally intensive finding (mining). The *XRP Ledger* can currently process 1,500 transactions per second, around the clock, and is easily scalable to over 65,000 transactions per second. This corresponds to the same throughput as Visa, for example.[38]

---

37   https://coinsutra.com/bitcoin-transfer-time/, retrieved: 05.12.2019
38   https://ripple.com/xrp/, retrieved: 05.12.2019

Bitcoin is a little more complicated. The block size is fixed and therefore only a limited number of transactions fit into one block. At the same time, a new block is created only every 10 minutes. If there are more transactions than can be processed, a traffic queue is created. Although you can now buy preferential processing with higher transaction fees, this makes it even less profitable for small transactions. Since the time required to confirm a payment also increases, the recipient may have to wait hours for the payment to be confirmed.[39]

Although there are various approaches to solving this problem, since there is rarely agreement on this within the Bitcoin community, inconsistent changes in the software code give rise to so-called forks (spin-offs), i.e. new versions of Bitcoin. This has happened several times in the past. Examples are **Litecoin**, **Bitcoin Cash** and **Bitcoin Gold**[40], which are also all still traded separately and have their own market value. A

---

39   https://www.btc-echo.de/der-preis-der-dezentralitaet-blockchain-und-skalierbarkeit/, retrieved: 05.12.2019
40   https://www.bitwala.com/de/5-bekannte-bitcoin-forks-die-du-2019-kennen-solltest/, retrieved: 05.12.2019

fork means that someone receives a forked version of the Bitcoins for free in addition to their Bitcoins. In the past, if the fork had enough followers, supply and demand even created value for the forked versions of Bitcoin, which was a pleasant money making experience out of nowhere. However, in the long term, this creates the danger of Bitcoin fragmentation into an infinite number of different versions.

Due to the obvious weaknesses of Bitcoin in terms of payment functionalities (medium of exchange), even many Bitcoin supporters see the main future benefit as a 'store of value', i.e. a form of investment with a value preserving function.

Power consumption / CO2 emissions

Certainly no one had given much thought to electricity consumption when Bitcoin was launched in 2009. For the mining of Bitcoin blocks as well as for the confirmation of transactions, cryptographic puzzles have to be solved, which are very computationally intensive. Like any other digital process, this costs energy and consumes power. Researchers from **Cambridge** have taken a closer look at the power consumption of the Bitcoin network and provide results updated every 30 seconds. They come up with an estimated power consumption of currently over **72 TWh per year**.[41] The site also provides comparative values directly. Currently, the annual power consumption of the Bitcoin network is between the total power consumption of Venezuela and Chili. The U.S. is ranked 2nd worldwide with 3,902 TWh electricity consumption.[42]

This hunger for electricity means that Bitcoin Mining tends to migrate to countries with cheap electricity, while in other countries, such as the U.S. or Germany, it is even unprofitable, as the cost of electricity including hardware was higher than the reward for mining and confirming transactions. *JPMorgan Chase & Co.* calculated that the average global mining costs in the 4th quarter of 2018 were USD 4,060. In China, in some cases only $2,400 and in other countries, such as Germany, significantly higher.[43]

---

41   https://www.cbeci.org/, retrieved: 05.12.2019
42   https://www.cbeci.org/comparisons/, retrieved: 05.12.2019
43   https://www.bloomberg.com/news/articles/2019-01-25/bitcoin-is-worth-less-

The power consumption in the *XRP* network is negligible. A member of the *XRP community* tried to calculated it exactly and came to 10,661 trees that would have to be planted to make *XRP* CO2 neutral[44]. For Bitcoin it would be 1,628,636,364 trees in the same period.

What is the regulatory framework?

Cryptocurrencies were and still are something new. Accordingly, to this day there is no globally unified regulatory framework, but rather a patchwork of different regulations.[45]

The big difference between Bitcoin and *XRP* is the way this regulatory vacuum is handled. Bitcoin could not actively seek contact with regulatory authorities worldwide due to the lack of a central authority. At the same time, it was also not in line with Bitcoin's philosophy to work proactively with regulators. Finally, Bitcoin's goal is to create an independent, decentralized

---

than-the-cost-to-mine-it-jpmorgan-says, retrieved: 05.12.2019
44   https://twitter.com/stedas/status/1147818712432611328, retrieved: 05.12.2019
45   https://en.wikipedia.org/wiki/Legality_of_bitcoin_by_country_or_territory, retrieved: 06.12.2019

financial system that cannot be manipulated politically. Bitcoin is to be its own central bank. That this vision is not in the interest of national governments, a threat to the conventional monetary system and thus to the state's monopoly on money, can be imagined. Therefore, time and again in various states, a ban on Bitcoin and other cryptocurrencies is being considered.

From a technical point of view, however, a ban in individual states is irrelevant, since precisely this is impossible in a decentralized cryptocurrency without a higher-level central authority. The focus is therefore on controlling the Bitcoin trade, which would make market access to Bitcoin, but also to other cryptocurrencies, much more difficult.

One can assume that states would do everything to secure their monopoly on money. You don't have to go back that far in history to find examples of this. In the 20th century, gold was banned in some democratic countries. These included the U.S. in 1933, France in 1936 and Great Britain in 1966. As late as 1973, private gold ownership was still subject to restrictions in more than 120 states around the world. In the U.S., the value limit for private gold holdings (except for jewellery and watches) was 100 US dollars in 1933. As a rule, the prohibitions had their origin in a currency crisis, e.g. triggered by high national debt, combined with a flight of capital from national currencies into supposedly safe investments such as gold, silver, platinum or foreign currencies.[46] Nowadays, in economic crises, the central banks usually react with low interest rates in order to expand the available money supply; this was not easily possible at that time, as one was subject to the **Gold Standard**, i.e. a central bank was only allowed to print as much money as one had as collateral in gold.[47]

Of course, the overall context was a little more complex, but it is not difficult to find parallels to the present day. The Gold Standard no longer exists, and the spiral of interest rate cuts to prevent an economic and financial crisis has already reached negative levels. While since the financial crisis of 2008 has subsided, the ever cheaper money has flowed into shares and

---

46   https://de.wikipedia.org/wiki/Goldverbot, retrieved: 06.12.2019
47   https://www.finanzen100.de/finanznachrichten/wirtschaft/krise-1933-als-praesident-roosevelt-den-gold-besitz-verbot_H1951016042_65256/, retrieved: 06.12.2019

real estate, as can be seen from the extremely sharp rise in share prices and real estate prices, in one or another country the next phase of capital flee could perhaps take place into cryptocurrencies, in order to remove the capital from an upcoming confiscation of the government to avert an economic crisis.

But what about *XRP*? Is a ban also being discussed here? The big advantage of *XRP* on the regulatory front is the interest of the company Ripple and other companies that want to use the *XRP Ledger* to have a clear regulatory framework, because it is essential for their business model and otherwise banks and other companies would not be allowed to use *XRP*. *Ripple* has therefore worked very closely with regulatory authorities and governments from the very beginning. It is not Ripple's goal to replace the existing financial system, but to complement it with *XRP* to and it more effective and more efficient.

Ripple has its own global team that works exclusively on worldwide regulatory matters. *Ripple* is also the only company in the cryptocurrency and blockchain scene that has opened its own office in Washington, D.C. for this purpose, and has included former regulatory executives on its board of directors.[48] In total, *Ripple* is actively working with 50 governments around the world to drive regulation of its business model, including *XRP*.[49]

Team, developers, partnerships and customers

Bitcoin is developed by a large community. In December 2019, the project had 679 contributors, people who made contributions to the software code.[50] Basically, anyone is allowed to submit new code or improvements to **GitHub** (that's where the software code resides). The changes are then discussed and voted on. Since there was often disagreement in the Bitcoin community, there were, as mentioned above, frequent spin-offs from Bitcoin. The official Bitcoin website is https://bitcoincore.org/.

According to Coinmap, there are currently more than 15,800

48   https://www.forbes.com/sites/jasonbrett/2019/10/22/ripple-expands-regulatory-strategy-in-washington-dc/#63197daa1eb4, retrieved: 06.12.2019

49   Digital Currency Regulation Around the World with Ripple's Michelle Bond, https://youtu.be/P1CMdNVFHI4, retrieved: 06.12.2019

50   https://github.com/bitcoin/bitcoin, retrieved: 06.12.2019

acceptance points for Bitcoin. The highest acceptance is in Central Europe, Great Britain, South Korea, Japan, Taiwan and the USA.[51]

The Bitcoin ecosystem is driven by specialized providers, such as **Bitpay**, which claims to be the leading global cryptocurrency payment service provider[52], who have established business models, especially based on Bitcoin payments. Business-to-business payments now account for more than 10% of all company transactions. *BitPay* researchers estimated that the average B2B payment in 2015 was around USD 2,500.00, 25 times higher than the average consumer payment of USD 100.00.[53] This also shows very clearly where profitable business models with Bitcoin could be found. It's not micropayments by consumers, for the reasons already mentioned above. This is probably the reason why *Bitpay* wants to introduce XRP payments at the end of 2019.[54]

---

51   https://coinmap.org/view/#/world/50.06419174/14.41406250/2, retrieved: 06.12.2019
52   https://bitpay.com/, retrieved: 06.12.2019
53   https://bitcoinonair.com/b2b-bitcoin-payments-on-rise-13802, retrieved: 06.12.2019
54   http://www.globenewswire.com/news-release/2019/10/02/1924157/0/en/ BitPay-Announces-Plans-to-Support-XRP-for-Payment-Processing-and-Cross-

Team, developers and contributors

The software code of *XRP* is also freely available on *Github*, but there are only 75 contributors.[55] Many of the contributors are employees of Ripple. The actual software, RippleNet, which makes use of the XRP Ledger, is not freely available. But since Ripple has a vested interest in selling the XRP Ledger as part of its software solution, more than 350 employees in six offices around the world are now available to sell the products, conduct active marketing and drive regulation in various markets.

Partnerships and customers

Ripple already has over 300 financial institutions in 40 countries as customers.[56] These include central banks, private banks, remittance companies, brokers, payment service providers, software companies and consulting firms. Not all of them are known, but you can get a good overview on this[57] unofficial site (http://rppl.info/). Another up-to-date overview is

---

Border-Transfers.html, retrieved: 06.12.2019
55   https://github.com/ripple/rippled, retrieved: 06.12.2019
56   https://ripple.com/customers/, retrieved: 06.12.2019
57   http://rppl.info/, retrieved: 10.12.2019

available here[58]. This makes *Ripple* almost the only company that offers Blockchain products in commercial use.[59]

Of the more than 300 customers, 37 companies are already using *XRP*, either as a payment method or to make international bank transfers. 24 of them already use On-Demand Liquidity (ODL)[60], which uses *XRP* in cross-border payment transactions.[61]

58 https://www.publish0x.com/xrp-community/full-list-ripple-customers-20192010-update-xmjwkg, retrieved: 06.12.2019
59 https://ripple.com/company/, retrieved: 06.12.2019
60 https://ripple.com/insights/ripplenet-growth-announcing-more-than-300-customers/, retrieved: 06.12.2019
61 https://dailyhodl.com/revealed-37-companies-now-using-xrp-with-24-launching-ripples-on-demand-liquidity/, retrieved: 06.12.2019

Chapter 2: Should I invest in XRP?

In the last chapter, I explained the differences between *XRP* and Bitcoin, highlighting why *XRP* is technologically superior to Bitcoin in many respects. *XRP* was actually not designed as a global currency, but rather as a global financial infrastructure, which is a fascinating approach.

Part of the fascination is that every new customer of *Ripple*, every new company that develops based on the *XRP Ledger*, every new digital currency that is issued (including Facebook Libra or digital currencies issued by governments (central banks) will potentially actively use *XRP* as a bridge currency to have the opportunity to be cheaply and quickly exchangeable worldwide into existing fiat currencies, other digital currencies or anything else that is traded.

This sounds like a solid use case for *XRP* and could lead to higher value. **David Schwartz**, the CTO of Ripple once gave an interesting answer to a user's question about this. The question was: "*If banks use Ripple for payments but don't need to buy XRP, who buys XRP and why should the price go up? Does it make sense to invest in XRP?*"

Part of the response was: "*We believe that we've build a payment system ("RippleNet") that's so much better than existing payment systems that banks will use it. But the payments still have to be settled somehow, and typically that's going to mean going through correspondent banks and nostro/vostro accounts. This is expensive and slow. As RippleNet grows, there will be more and more payments that have no technical obstacles to being settled by XRP instead of the slow, old way. Then as we make XRP work for those corridors (as we've already done with xRapid for USD/MXN) those payments can easily settle through XRP... If we're successful with this strategy, and XRP is used as a settlement currency for some fraction of RippleNet payments, that could set up sources of demand for XRP.....*" Higher demand usually goes hand in hand with a higher price.

The complete answer can be found here: https://qr.ae/TZZ3er

By the way, that was in 2018, after the price of *XRP* had risen 37,000% within a year in 2017. On January 4, 2018, the price reached its all-time high of USD 3.65 on at least one exchange. Shortly before that, Bitcoin also reached its all-time high of almost USD 20,000. Quite a few of those who already had *XRP* in their portfolios at the beginning of 2017 suddenly became crypto-millionaires. But just as many who bought or held XRP at that time also experienced the price drop to currently around USD 0.22. Again, it was all cryptocurrencies that lost up to 90% of their all-time high. The price is currently still dominated by speculators and not by fundamental key figures or the benefits of a cryptocurrency. This shows the current risk of an investment into cryptocurrencies.

Bitcoin has always played a crucial role in this process, as Bitcoin currently dominates the entire market. The current market dominance is still over 66%.[62] This also shows how immature the crypto market still is and that it is not yet the companies behind the crypto currencies with their innovative problem solutions that determine the value, but rather the hype behind the blockchain technology itself and thus behind the still best known crypto currency, namely Bitcoin. Although from a technological point of view, as I have introduced elsewhere, Bitcoin is rather outdated technology.

It reminded me very much of the dotcom bubble at the millennium. Millions are flowing into companies that only mentioned the word "Internet" in their business plan. A few survived with a good professional business model and a focus on solving real customer problems. It's the same now. The crypto companies who have real customers and solve real problems will survive. There are very few of them now. *Ripple* is one of them, with over 300 real customers already.

---

62   https://coinmarketcap.com/de/charts/, retrieved: 09.12.2019

When is the right time for an investment?

From the development of all cryptocurrencies including *XRP* in 2017-2019, one can see that it is very difficult to find the right time for an investment, especially when the markets are still dominated by speculators. These speculators make the markets, they do not react to them. The ones who react are the traders who try to read the probabilities for an up or down in short term charts. Most of them probably lose more money than they gain. Most of them are gamblers.

In principle, "do your own research" applies, research before you make an investment decision. It is also always good to diversify, not only within one asset class, but across several asset classes. If you are not just another speculative trader who wants to make (or lose) the quick money, but are interested in a longer-term investment or even in a addition to your pension plan, then "**HODL**" is the right strategy for you.

HODL is a meme well known in the crypto scene. It stands for people's ability to persevere, even if the cryptocurrency falls significantly. HODL was born on December 18, 2013, due to a spelling mistake made by the somewhat drunk user "*GameKyyubi*" in a <u>forum post</u> on BitcoinTalk.org, when the Bitcoin course suddenly crashed. The title of his post was "I AM HODLING"[63]. The Bitcoin price had risen from around USD 13 to over USD 1,000 in 2013 and then dropped back to around USD 400 within a few days in December.

When you consider that the Bitcoin price had reached almost USD 20,000 at the end of 2017, you realize how difficult it is to decide on the right entry or exit point. If you don't want to look at the prices all the time, the best strategy is to create a well sorted portfolio and then hold it for the long term. If you are already close to retirement, slightly less volatile forms of investment are recommended.

In general, it should be noted that cryptocurrencies, like other forms of investment, often move in cycles. So it tends to be better not to enter at the all-time high, but when many others exit due to sharply falling prices. From this perspective, it is now more attractive to buy *XRP* than on January 4, 2018, when

---

63   https://bitcointalk.org/index.php?topic=375643.0, retrieved: 12.10.2019

XRP was at its all-time high of USD 3.65. But that is something that everyone has to decide for themselves.

How high can the price of XRP rise?

Unfortunately, there is no general answer to this question and any price forecast you read on the Internet is as good as reading tea leaves.

There are basically two main factors that influence the price. On the one hand it is speculation. This has controlled the price almost exclusively until today. On the other hand, there is the use of *XRP*, i.e. the minimum value that *XRP* must have in order to fulfil its function as a bridge currency.

Only the *XRPs* that are in the so-called circulating supply can fulfil this bridge function.[64] This is currently about 43 billion XRP out of the existing 100 billion *XRP*. Not in circulation are the 55 billion XRP *Ripple* has in an electronic escrow account and all *XRP* that are not on trading exchanges but in private wallets.

---

64   https://coinmarketcap.com/currencies/xrp/markets/, retrieved: 12.10.2019

As mentioned above, Ripple's two mentioned use cases alone require a total liquidity of almost 7 trillion USD per day. In addition, there are all the other use cases that have already been technically implemented, e.g. streaming payments and virtual goods in the gaming sector (I will come to this again in the next chapter).

However, if you think about the vision of "*Internet of Value*", at some point in time it is basically any value that could be swapped for any other value through XRP liquidity. This also includes

- other cryptocurrrencies and digital assets that are transferred worldwide
- digital currencies issued by states in the future
- Gold and other precious metals
- Diamonds and other precious stones
- Bonus miles and coupons
- and so on…

You can already see that the future importance of a bridge currency is only limited by the question of how big you can think - that is, your imagination. This is also reflected in this illustrative graphic "All of the World's Money and Markets in One Visualization".[65]

Nobody can say how high the market share the XRP Ledger can achieve as part of a future financial infrastructure and when how much liquidity has to be provided by it, but it could be an interesting bet for the future.

---

65 http://money.visualcapitalist.com/worlds-money-markets-one-visualization-2017/, retrieved: 10.12.2019

Chapter 3: Buying, sending and securely storing XRP

Maybe your interest in *XRP* has increased in the meantime. In this chapter I will explain how and where you can buy *XRP* and how you can store it safely.

How to buy and store XRP and other cryptocurrencies?

There are several ways to participate in the *XRP* course. I will only go into detail on the alternatives which include a real "physical" purchase of *XRP*.

There is now also the possibility to buy Contracts for Difference (CFDs) or certificates of many crypto currencies. These allow you to participate in the price development (also with leverage), but you never own "physical" *XRP*. Well-known providers include Plus500[66] and eToro[67]. But be careful, CFDs are complex financial instruments and quite a few people

---

66   https://www.plus500.de/, retrieved: 10.12.2019
67   https://www.etoro.com/, retrieved: 10.12.2019

lose money here.

Even in 2017 it was not so easy to buy *XRP* directly with EURO. The usual way was to buy Bitcoin or Ethereum and with that you bought other crypto currencies, like XRP. Fortunately this has changed. Today you can buy *XRP* without problems directly against EURO. Some possibilities I introduce further down.

How do I keep my XRP and other cryptocurrencies safe?

However, before you buy *XRP*, you should consider where to store it safely. You will need a so-called "wallet" (electronic purse). It is not recommended to leave crypto currencies purchased on a crypto wallet there permanently, especially if you are dealing with larger amounts. From my own experience I can confirm that it would not be the first time that a wallet has been hacked and many investors would have lost some or all of their deposits. Many crypto-trading exchanges now have insurance, but it's just not worth the trouble and you don't have real control over your *XRP* until you have the private key. This is only guaranteed with your own wallet.

What is a private key?

When a new wallet is created, two keys are generated, a private and a public key. These are mathematically linked together. The public key is, simply put, your wallet address/XRP address (it looks something like this: rDbWJ9C7uExThZYAwV8m6LsZ5YSX3sa6US). The address can be passed on without fear. The private key, however, is the "PIN" to access the wallet. Whoever has the private key has full access to your crypto currencies.

There are different types of wallets - hardware wallets, software wallets, mobile wallets, online wallets, paper wallets. I will not introduce them all in this introduction. Most people use hardware wallets today because it is the easiest and most convenient way to securely store your *XRPs* or other cryptocurrencies offline and keep them out of hackers' reach. I myself use the **Ledger Nano S**, the most common hardware wallet, which I would like to introduce here. Storing offline does not mean that you download your *XRP* (or other cryptocurrencies). *XRPs* cannot leave their *XRP Ledger*. What you store offline are the private keys you need for each transaction.

Hardware-Wallet - Ledger Nano S

The Ledger Nano S is something like a USB stick with special features. I recommend to order the Ledger Nano S only on the official website and definitely not to buy used ones anywhere. The danger is much too great that someone has already copied the private keys assigned to the Ledger Nano S.

If you order via this **link**[68] (or QR Code), I will receive a small commission for the referral. The Ledger Nano S is not cheap, but it is definitely worth its money.

Once you have your new Ledger Nano S at home and unpacked, simply visit the following website

---

68   https://www.ledgerwallet.com/r/2e64?path=/products/ledger-nano-s

(https://www.ledger.com/start/) and follow the steps one by one. For example, you will also need the Ledger Live software[69], which allows you to view your *XRP* and send and receive *XRP*. If you have difficulties with the setup, just have a look at some videos on *YouTube*. Then it works for sure.

When you're done setting up the *Ledger Nano S*, you can start out in a good conscience and buy your first *XRP*. You'll find out how to do that in a moment.

By the way, if your *Ledger Nano S* is lost or destroyed, your *XRPs* are **not** gone. As long as you don't lose the card with the 24 words you created when you set up your *Ledger Nano S*, you can restore your *XRP* wallet on a newly purchased *Ledger Nano S*. Your private key is encoded in the 24 words.

Where and how can you buy XRP ?

There are basically three ways to buy XRP:

■ Directly from the *XRP Ledger* with EURO from your

---

69   https://www.ledger.com/ledger-live/, retrieved: 10.12.2019

IBAN-Account (On-Ledger)

- On a crypto trading exchange
- From an innovative financial services provider

Buy XRP directly from the XRP Ledger with EURO from your IBAN-Account (On-Ledger)

As I mentioned in a previous chapter, the *XRP Ledger* has an integrated crypto trading exchange, which the *XRP Ledger* needs to exchange between any currencies in real time. For example, if someone sends US dollars to Mexico. The US dollars are then automatically converted into *XRP* and then automatically exchanged into Mexican pesos in Mexico. This happens on the exchange built into the *XRP Ledger* and of course you can also buy *XRP* directly from the built-in exchange.

Update 02/14/2020: The tool XRPARROT introduced below is currently no longer available for regulatory reasons.[70] In the hope that a solution can be found quickly, I will not delete the following paragraph yet.

---

70 https://twitter.com/WietseWind/status/1217819942801809408, retrieved: 14.02.2020

An excellent tool for this is **_XRPARROT_**[71], which **Wietse Wind**, a Dutch developer and XRP enthusiast, has developed along with many other great tools. He is an active member of the *XRP community* and has already gained the attention of *Ripple* through his commitment and ideas for the development of the *XRP* ecosystem. Since 2019, he has been developing full-time for the *XRP Ledger*[72], which was made possible by an investment[73] from **_Xpring_**.[74] *Xpring* is a *Ripple* initiative, founded in May 2018, which promotes companies and projects that share and develop the vision of the *Internet of Value (IoV)*.[75]

You can use XRPARROT for *XRP* purchases up to 2,000 EUR per month. To purchase via XRPARROT, all you need is the XRP wallet address of your ledger Nano S, your IBAN (the account to be debited from your XRP purchase) and a mobile

71   https://www.xrparrot.com/, retrieved: 06.12.2019
72   https://wietse.com/bio, retrieved: 06.12.2019
73   https://medium.com/xpring/investing-in-wietse-winds-xrpl-labs-cff19d964c76, retrieved: 06.12.2019
74   https://medium.com/xpring/investing-in-wietse-winds-xrpl-labs-cff19d964c76, retrieved: 06.12.2019
75   https://ripple.com/insights/welcome-to-xpring/, retrieved: 06.12.2019

phone number.

It is important to note that a new wallet (*XRP address*), including the one on your *Ledger Nano S*, is not immediately active. It only activates when you have sent at least 20 *XRP* to it. This is the so-called account reserve. This one-time fee is required by the *XRP Ledger* network and is not refundable. They remain on the *XRP* wallet address forever. However, this reserve can theoretically change if, for example, *XRP* increases in value significantly.

Your *XRP* wallet address will be displayed when you connect your *Ledger Nano S* to your computer, log on to the *Ledger Nano S* with your PIN and switch to the *XRP* wallet on the *Ledger Nano S*. To do this, you have to open the *Ledger Live software* on your computer. If you now click on the "Receive" link, your *XRP* receiving address (i.e. your *XRP* wallet address) will be displayed. It should always be the same, since it is assigned to your Ledger Nano S. As in the example above, the *XRP* wallet address usually starts with a small "r". In rare cases, it may start with a capital "X". Enter the *XRP* destination address on XRPARROT together with your IBAN and your mobile phone number. Just follow the instructions here[76] (https://www.xrparrot.com/sendxrp) and everything will work. As soon as XRPARROT has received your money from your IBAN account, the XRP will automatically be credited to your *XRP wallet.* You will be informed by SMS. The next time you look into your *XRP* wallet from your *Ledger Nano S* via *Ledger Live,* they will be displayed.

If you only want to look at your *XRP* wallet, you can also do this online. It is a pseudonymous blockchain, i.e. anyone can view any transaction and any *XRP* wallet address, but does not know who it belongs to. You can find a good *XRP* explorer here[77]: https://bithomp.com/explorer/.

If you want to buy *XRP* for more than EUR 2,000 per month, you have to buy it through another channel. For example, via a crypto trading exchange.

---

76   https://www.xrparrot.com/sendxrp, retrieved: 10.12.2019
77   https://bithomp.com/explorer/, retrieved: 10.12.2019

Buy XRP from a crypto trading exchange

There are now countless crypto trading exchanges. At the beginning I would recommend using a crypto trading exchange that allows direct payment of the XRP against FIAT currency, e.g. EURO or US Dollar and/or credit card payment. Sometimes the fees are a bit higher, but it is the easiest way and you will have the fastest results. There are many exchanges that offer the purchase of *XRP* only against Bitcoin (BTC) or Ethereum (ETH). which was the normal way a few years ago. But this makes buying more complicated. Depending on the country, the sale of the BTC or ETH might directly result in a taxable event. A good overview of the worldwide XRP/FIAT pairings can be found on the following page[78].

For Europeans it makes sense to choose one that accepts SEPA transfers and at the same time allows to buy *XRP* directly against EURO. Instead of SEPA transfers, credit card or PayPal payments are also often accepted. These are faster, but usually the fees are much higher. Since SEPA transfers usually take a maximum of one day, you can save the

---

78   https://www.xrparcade.com/xrpfiatpairs/ retrieved: 22.12.2019

additional fees. How long it takes in individual cases depends on your bank. With Deutsche Bank, for example, it has always taken about 24 hours, while ING has often made it in about four hours. If your bank offers real time transfers, it may even be quicker, but there may be some additional fees.

A good selection of crypto trading exchanges can be found here[79] (https://ripple.com/xrp/buy-xrp/). I myself have made good experiences with Bitstamp[80], Bittrex[81] and Coinbase[82] (Affiliate-Link). These (esp. Coinbase) have a very good user experience and usability and therefore they are also very suitable for beginners.

Before you can get started, you have to go through a somewhat complex registration and verification process for security and legal reasons. But everything is explained step-by-step and there are also excellent instructions on YouTube. You should also directly activate the **2-factor-authentication**. You

79   https://ripple.com/xrp/buy-xrp/, retrieved: 07.12.2019
80   https://www.bitstamp.net/, retrieved: 07.12.2019
81   https://global.bittrex.com/, retrieved: 07.12.2019
82   https://www.coinbase.com/join/podzus_f, (Affiliate-Link) retrieved:
     07.12.2019

need something like this when you log in to your online account. It usually works via the **Google Authenticator App**.

Once you have completed the registration process, select the links to "Deposit" or deposit. There you will find out what you have to do for a EURO SEPA transfer to the exchange.

When your money has been received on the exchange, it will be displayed and you can buy *XRP* for EURO. There are several options, according to which rules you can execute an order or a purchase. If you have no experience with the different ways of buying, choose "Instant Order" on Bitstamp. No options are offered on Coinbase.

Your purchased *XRP* are available immediately after purchase, so you can send them directly to your Ledger Nano S for safe storage. See below to find out how to send XRP. First, I will explain the third way to buy *XRP* - from an innovative financial service provider.

Buy XRP from an innovative financial services provider (Fintech)

Fintechs are companies that often provide various innovative services with optimized customer experience. For example, an own IBAN account with Maestro card (if you are in Europe), credit cards and the direct purchase option of different crypto currencies. All combined in an attractive app or on an online platform.

Uphold

Uphold[83] is a London-based company and has been in existence since 2015, where you can buy over 30 different currencies, cryptocurrencies, but also gold, for example. You can send the *XRP* you buy there without any restrictions, for example to your *Ledger Nano S*. *Uphold* can be used as an app as well as on any desktop computer.

Bison App

Bison App[84] is an app for buying crypto-currencies of the Stuttgart stock exchange. The company behind it is SOWA

---

83   https://uphold.com/, retrieved: 08.12.2019
84   https://bisonapp.com/de-de/, retrieved: 11.12.2019

Labs, which is a spin-off of a European research project.[85] Currently, only bank transfers are accepted as a payment method. The fees are quite reasonable. There are currently four cryptocurrencies offered Bitcoin, Ethereum, Litecoin and *XRP*, and a transfer to your own wallet is possible.

Revolut

Another good app to buy *XRP* instantly is Revolut. But I will not go into detail about it, because you can only send *XRP* bought there to other Revolut users, e.g. not to your Ledger Nano S. That means you do not have the private keys of your *XRPs*, so you do not have 100% control. As soon as they have added functionality, Revolut is definitely a recommendation.

How to send or transfer XRP?

You have now successfully bought *XRP*, but they are not yet on your *Ledger Nano S* for secure storage. To get them there, you will need to send/transfer them from where you bought them to your *Ledger Nano S*. If you bought *XRP* from *XRPARROT*, this is not necessary, as you had directly entered

---

85   https://www.sowalabs.com/, retrieved: 11.12.2019

the *XRP* address of your *Ledger Nano S* as recipient address.

To send your *XRP* from the crypto trading exchange to your *Ledger Nano S*, simply follow the instructions within the exchange. You will need the recipient address of your *Ledger Nano S*, which usually starts with a small "r". You enter this as the destination address in the crypto trading exchange. If you send your *XRP* to your *Ledger Nano S*, you **don't need** a destination tag. You only need this tag if you send your *XRP* to a crypto trading exchange, because the exchanges store all *XRP* on the same *XRP* address. The *destination tag* is the differentiation criteria for the mapping to the respective owner. So you should never forget to specify it when sending *XRP* to a stock exchange, if you don't want to have long discussions with customer service.

So, now that you are hopefully the proud owner of *XRPs*, you might want to meet other people who share the same interest as you. The *XRP* universe and especially the *XRP* community is big, helpful and mostly very likeable. You will get to know them in the next chapter.

Chapter 4: The Ripple and XRP Universe

XRP now has one of the most active and largest communities in the crypto world and the *XRP* universe is growing rapidly. Not only by *Ripple*, but by many companies that offer solutions based on the *XRP Ledger* how to send values worldwide in real time.

All these companies and people are united by an understanding of the long-term potential of the technology and the solutions based on it. In particular, *Ripple*, which has positioned the vision of moving values worldwide in the future in the same way that information is moved in the market today, has been the driving force behind the development over the last few years.

The *XRP* universe with its community and affiliated companies uses all available social channels and is predominantly English-speaking, as long as you are not in asia.

I will introduce the individual channels, but I will also pick out a few people who have earned the respect of the *XRP* community through their commitment and sometimes they serve several channels.

Who should you follow on Twitter?

Twitter has established itself as the basic communication channel for everything around *Ripple* and *XRP*. You should at least follow the following people if you want to be well informed at all times. I have partly completed the self introduction of the persons of Twitter.

Ripple @Ripple[86]

Instantly move money to all corners of the world.

Brad Garlinghouse @bgarlinghouse[87]

CEO at Ripple

David Schwartz @JoelKatz[88]

Improving global settlement with blockchain tech. CTO at Ripple; one of the original architects of the XRP network. All

---

86   https://twitter.com/Ripple, retrieved: 09.12.2019
87   https://twitter.com/bgarlinghouse, retrieved: 09.12.2019
88   https://twitter.com/JoelKatz, retrieved: 09.12.2019

tweets are off the record.

Bank XRP @BankXRP[89]

My interests are banks, bank software, blockchain, fintechs, IoV, IoT, R3, Ripple, coil, IPL, Interledger

Nordic Ann @NordicAnn[90]

XRP enthusiast and so much more.

Hodor @Hodor[91]

I also follow all things Fintech*XRP*IoV*Coil*ILP. I especially ♥#xrp, I blog at Coil and at the XRP Community Blog

Ethan Beard @ethanbeard[92]

Leading #Xpring at @Ripple. Building the #XRP and crypto ecosystem.

89   https://twitter.com/BankXRP, retrieved: 09.12.2019
90   https://twitter.com/nordicann, retrieved: 09.12.2019
91   https://twitter.com/hodor, retrieved: 09.12.2019
92   https://twitter.com/ethanbeard, retrieved: 09.12.2019

Alex Cobb @AlexCobb_ [93]

Bereits 2017 Videos aus dem Kinderzimmer. Auch auf YouTube: Alex Cobb

Evan Schwartz @_emschwartz [94]

Co-Inventor of @interledger, focused on building the Interledger community and http://interledger.rs, engineering lead at @XpringDev / @Ripple.

Adrian Hope-Bailie @ahopebailie [95]

Head of @Interledger at @Coil, Co-chair @W3C Web Payments WG. Building the Internet of Value.

Tiffany Hayden @haydentiff [96]

One of the most important contributors of Ripple and XRP with close connections to Ripple.

---

93 https://twitter.com/AlexCobb_, retrieved: 09.12.2019
94 https://twitter.com/_emschwartz, retrieved: 09.12.2019
95 https://twitter.com/ahopebailie, retrieved: 09.12.2019
96 https://twitter.com/haydentiff, retrieved: 09.12.2019

C3|Nik @C3_Nik[97]

News & opinions on #Crypto and #FinancialMarkets. I am an investor, not a worshipper. Engaging in research, not hype.

Wietse Wind @WietseWind[98]

Building on the XRP Ledger. Er ist auch der Entwickler von XRPARROT und XRPTIPBOT.

CryptoEri @sentosumosaba[99]

Regular Crypto Updates with an emphasis on what impacts this space. Attention paid to the top 20 assets by market cap with special focus on XRP.

Beware of Twitter scammers

If you're on Twitter, watch out for fake and malicious Twitter accounts posing as influential members of the community or actual *Ripple* employees. These accounts scam crypto owners. Usually you can recognize them by the fact that they promise free XRP e.g. in the sense of send me 100 *XRP*

---

97   https://twitter.com/C3_Nik, retrieved: 09.12.2019
98   https://twitter.com/wietsewind, retrieved: 09.12.2019
99   https://twitter.com/sentosumosaba, retrieved: 09.12.2019

and you win 1000 *XRP*... or they offer a giveaway...

Basic rule in social media: If it sounds too good to be true, there is probably a fraudulent intent behind it.

What are popular YouTuber for Ripple and XRP?

I would like to highlight the following YouTubers in particular:

- Ripple
- Alex Cobb
- Digital Asset Investor
- crypto Eri
- BankXRP
- Jungle Inc
- DM Logic's XRPhilosophy
- To The Lifeboats
- CKJ Crypto News
- Brad Kimes
- DustyBC
- Working Money Channel

- Kevin Cage

- OZ Crypto

- Michael Zischeck

- Esoteric Trading Solutions Teaching Crypto Markets

There are many other great people who regularly contribute valuable content to the *XRP community*. If you get a little more active, you will automatically find the people who are most relevant to you. If you think someone is missing, just let me know (e.g. by sending me a message via Twitter @arndt_gg).

What other channels are used? XRPChat, Reddit, etc.

More in-depth discussions about Ripple and XRP take place on two channels in particular:

- XRP Chat[100]: https://www.xrpchat.com/
- Reddit:
    - Ripple: https://www.reddit.com/r/Ripple/ (207.000

---

100 https://www.xrpchat.com/, retrieved: 09.12.2019

members)

- XRP: https://www.reddit.com/r/XRP/ (39.200 members)

Further various community channels can be found on Discord and Telegram. Since this usually requires invitations, I have not linked them. If you become an active member of the community, you will automatically receive invitations.

What other interesting content about Ripple and XRP is available?

- https://xrpcommunity.blog/ - from the XRP community for the XRP community
- https://www.stedas.hr/index-en.html - many infographics on Ripple and XRP
- https://www.xrparcade.com/ - "everything about *XRP*" the website promises
- https://coil.com/u/Hodor - Hodor's *XRP* Blog - No. 1 blogger about XRP
- https://fudbingo.com/ - provides answers to the most common misunderstandings about XRP. FUD stands for

71

"fear, uncertainty, doubt". It is usually used by groups or individuals to deliberately misinform others.

In addition to the activities in the *XRP community*, there are also companies and services that are actively involved in the further development of the *XRP* ecosystem and thus want to promote the realization of the *Internet of Value*. In the following I introduce some of them:

What is the Interledger Protocol (ILP) and why is it so important?

Interledger is an open protocol suite for sending payments across different ledgers/blockchains.[101] It therefore connects different ledgers/blockchains. Ripple played a major role in developing this protocol[102] and then made sure that development continues under the W3C umbrella. The W3C - World Wide Web Consortium is the committee for standardization of techniques in the World Wide Web.[103] There

---

101 https://interledger.org/, retrieved: 09.12.2019
102 https://ripple.com/insights/implementing-the-interledger-protocol/, retrieved: 14.12.2019
103 https://de.wikipedia.org/wiki/World_Wide_Web_Consortium, retrieved: 09.12.2019

is also a Web Payment Group below the W3C[104], which takes care of standardization and implementation in the existing web infrastructure, e.g. support of current browsers for payments. Everyone who is anyone is involved here.[105] If you are interested in what Ripple, the inventor of the Interledger Protocol, had to say about it in 2016, you can read it here.[106]

What is Xpring?

Xpring is a Ripple initiative founded in May 2018 to support companies and projects that share and develop the vision of the Internet of Value (IoV).[107] *Xpring* defines itself as the open platform for money, offering developers tools, services and programs to integrate "money" into applications.[108]

The Xpring Platform is entirely based on open source technology. The technologies used include:

---

104   https://www.w3.org/Payments/WG/, retrieved: 09.12.2019
105   https://www.w3.org/2004/01/pp-impl/83744/status, retrieved: 09.12.2019
106   https://ripple.com/insights/interledger-beyond-blockchain/, retrieved: 09.12.2019
107   https://ripple.com/insights/welcome-to-xpring/, retrieved: 06.12.2019
108   https://xpring.io/, retrieved: 09.12.2019

- *XRP* - for fast and inexpensive transfer of values. Decentralized, liquid and available everywhere
- INTERLEDGER PROTOCOL (ILP) - a standardized open protocol to simplify payments in any currency and with XRP as a real-time bridge currency
- WEB MONETIZATION - an open standard that allows content producers to get paid for consuming the content very easily.

The *Xpring* platform was basically built for every developer, but at the moment they are concentrating on some use cases:

- INVESTMENTS - wallets and exchanges
- CONTENT - Monetization of content producers
- GAMING - Owning and trading virtual goods with others

In the summer of 2019, *Xpring* announced that they had already invested $500 million in 20 companies within one year. 100 million US dollars of this was specifically targeted at gaming content.[109]

What is Coil?

Coils mission is to build an ecosystem of content suppliers, developers, businesses and non-profit organizations that use *XRP* to pay for content that uses the open standard "Web Monetization". The goal is to replace ad-supported content and subscription models.[110]

The keyword here is "streaming payments". Users pay a predetermined amount in real time per second or according to the progress of their reading, which can be a fraction of a cent.

Coil has successfully completed a USD 4 million financing round and in addition *Ripple* has provided them with 1 billion *XRP*. In June 2019, Coil invested $20 million in Imgur, a meme and storytelling app that has more than 300 million monthly users.[111]

---

109 https://www.ledgerinsights.com/xrp-ripple-xpring-invests-260-million-coil-content/, retrieved: 09.12.2019

110 https://www.ledgerinsights.com/xrp-ripple-xpring-invests-260-million-coil-content/, retrieved: 09.12.2019

111 https://imgur.com/gallery/SrrsEsN, retrieved: 09.12.2019

What other offerings are there in the XRP universe?

- https://www.cinnamon.video/ - a video platform with monetisation via coil

- https://www.xrptipbot.com/ - "XRP Tip Bot" is an automated program that allows users on Reddit, Twitter & Discord to send XRP to each other via comments or tweets.

- https://www.xrparrot.com/ - is a service that allows you to buy XRP directly through your IBAN account.

What role does Codius play in Smart Contracts?

Codius is the protocol developed by Ripple for the implementation of "Smart Contracts". Anyone who has ever used a vending machine knows Smart Contract. You put in a certain amount of money and then you get your desired product. Nothing else are Smart Contracts on the Internet. They are programmed events when certain conditions are met or payments are received.

Smart Contracts have long been a particular strength of Ethereum. With *Codius*, *Ripple* is now competing directly with

Ethereum and even with a small advantage. *Codius* supports various programming languages that developers usually already know, while Smart Contracts on Ethereum require their own programming language.

How can I get crypto loans with my XRP?

Various companies now offer the possibility to borrow on their *XRP*, i.e. to get a loan on it directly without having to sell it first. This makes sense for two reasons. Firstly, one continues to profit from a possible rise in the price of the cryptocurrency in time and secondly, there is no taxable sale if one does not own his cryptocurrency for at least a year. (might be country specific!). The latter can of course be positive as well, as long as you realize losses. I can't give any information about the exact tax effects, because I am not a tax consultant. Please be sure to consult your tax consultant before each sale.

If you decide to borrow your *XRP*, this is quite easily possible. You simply send your *XRP* to an *XRP* address provided by the provider and immediately receive a credit line, which you can also use directly. Everything takes only a few seconds, since *XRP* are transferable in real time. You can then transfer the money directly to your bank account, for example, by SEPA transfer.

Known providers are e.g.

- YouHodler: https://app.youhodler.com/
- Nexo: https://nexo.io/de
- Cred: https://mycred.io/

As with all online offerings that deal with financial matters, the registration and verification process is somewhat more complex for security reasons.

New offerings are coming onto the market almost daily to meet specific needs and/or provide an enhanced customer experience. The market does not stand still, but continues to develop at breathtaking speed. So it remains exciting.

Conclusion

We live in times of dynamic exponential technological progress. Everything is changing at an incredible rate. The same is true for the content in this publication. If you would like to be informed about updates, just send me an e-mail to xrp@podzus.de. I will then add you to the mailing list.

While the technological infrastructure to implement the *Internet of Value* is already available, the biggest challenge is to harmonize the different regulatory frameworks around the world as much as possible, just as the Information Internet has done in recent years.

A particular future trend is tokenization. More and more values are being converted into digital equivalents. In theory, everything can be converted into a token, whether it be material goods such as real estate, cars or jewellery, or immaterial goods such as shares, property rights or ideas. Through tokenization, everything becomes tradable, "securitized" in a token that is assigned to a blockchain that stores the current ownership in an non manipulable way.[112] In the long term, this will also affect our cash.

But this also means that the global trading volume of assets will grow exponentially, because theoretically everything is tradable against each other, as long as a bridge currency like *XRP* is established. We would then have a fully automated barter economy 4.0.

---

112 https://www.btc-echo.de/so-veraendert-die-tokenisierung-unser-finanzwesen-und-nicht-zuletzt-unser-leben/, retrieved: 11.12.2019

About the author

My digitization journey began in 1994 with the book "Internet" by Oliver Kortendick and Thomas Franke.

I still own this book today. On the back of the book it says: "As the largest networked system, the Internet offers you unimagined possibilities for electronic communication, data and program exchange, as well as access to a huge treasure of information. Up to now, these possibilities have been available in Germany almost exclusively at universities and for affiliated companies. Now you too can bring the world into your living room." That sounded great and all I needed was a PC with MS-DOS (version 3.3 or higher), a modem and a telephone connection.

There I sat in my 10m² student dormitory in Cologne at my 286 AT PC with 20 MB hard disk and went through the step-by-step instructions. What happened then should change my life forever. Slowly the library directory of the University of California was building up in front of me. At that moment I thought: "Wow, here I am sitting in my room in Cologne and at the same time I am on a computer in California." I knew this was the future. It is this enthusiasm and curiosity that still drives me every day to try out new things and explore the potential.

Professionally, I also dealt intensively with digital things already during my studies of business administration. I have created and operated my own portals, e.g. for package tours and cruises, and provided users through search engine optimization, built e-commerce portals in the RTL Group, was responsible for the classifieds portal at kalaydo.de and set up performance marketing, designed digital touchpoints such as websites, apps and multi-channel campaigns for a large pharmaceutical company, created the digital strategy for

Cologne Bonn Airport and advised and supported companies on topics related to the digital transformation.

I came to cryptocurrencies in 2017 when I read the biography of Elon Musk[113] (a book I highly recommend). He had and has the vision "that mankind must become a multi-planetary species". The background for this is the given probability that our planet could at some point become completely or partially uninhabitable due to one or more existentially threatening events. One of these existential risks is, for example, the escalating global warming, which Elon Musk would like to actively address through his activities in Tesla and SolarCity. At the same time, with SpaceX he is pursuing the foundation for future space flights in order to further pursue the vision of the multi-planetary species.

A major challenge in fighting such global risks is to

---

113   Elon Musk: How the Billionaire CEO of SpaceX and Tesla is Shaping our
       Future, https://amzn.to/396tNjx (Affiliate-Link)

decide on the right course of action, while avoiding the influence of short-term national political interests. Without going into the details now, blockchain technology would also be a suitable vehicle for global decentralized decision-making processes. When analyzing the possible applications of blockchain technology, I first came across Bitcoin and later to other cryptocurrencies, such as *Ripple* with *XRP*. Especially *Ripple* and *XRP* with the vision of the "*Internet of Value*" still inspire me on a daily basis.

Printed in Great Britain
by Amazon

13871878R00050